JAMES R. DORSETT

Evidence in the Web

An Unconventional Conversation About Science, Creation, and the Love of God

First published by Janna Publications LLC 2025

Second edition

ISBN: 979-8-218-94906-8

To our grandson, Sean

"Tune your ears to wisdom, and concentrate on understanding." (Prv. 2:2, NLT)

"He has also set eternity in the human heart; yet no one can fathom what God has done from beginning to end."
— Ecclesiastes 3:11 (NIV)

"The most incomprehensible thing about the universe is that it is comprehensible."
— Albert Einstein

Table of Contents

Acknowledgments		ii
Prologue		1
Introduction		2
1	Bitten!	3
2	Gettin' Schooled by an Arachnid	7
3	Engineering Marvels and Divine Design	11
4	The Question of LOVE	16
5	The Web of Silk	21
6	Quantum Physics and the Ultimate Observer	26
7	The Fall and Its Cosmic Consequences	34
8	The Plan for Redemption	42
9	EPILOGUE	49
10	NOTES	55

Acknowledgments

To my lovely wife, Anna, whose continued encouragement was vital for me to press through the challenges along the way. Also, thank you to all whose kind feedback and advice ensured I stay on the right path. And a special thanks to my daughter, Nicole, and my long-time friend, Keith, who provided special insights that helped make *Evidence in the Web* possible.

Prologue

It wasn't the first time I'd taken a stroll in one of the many parks in my neighborhood, enjoying the time alone with nature, nor the first time I'd contemplated the makings of the universe and its complexities. The air was still, the leaves barely rustled, and the sun filtered through the trees as though hinting at something deep and personal it wanted to share.

I wasn't ten minutes into my walk when I noticed the web—an intricate spiral spun with such precision that even an architect would have paused in awe. And at the center: an orb-weaving spider, legs extended, gently pulsing, waiting. Watching.

Maybe it was the stillness, maybe shimmering sunlight, or maybe—just maybe—it was the fact that I was beginning to suspect the answers I sought might be found in creation by means of this interesting arthropod and its surroundings. But whatever the reason, when it spoke, I wasn't surprised.

"It's a conundrum, isn't it?"

I looked around. No one else. Just me. And the web.

"What is?" I whispered.

"Everything," it replied. "But let's start with the web."

If you had told me I was about to explore the origins of the universe or the meaning of reality with an arachnid, I might've laughed. But I didn't. I listened.

Because, deep down, I'd been waiting for this conversation for most of my life.

Introduction

Dear Reader,

This book is not a sermon. It's not a defense of organized religion, nor a rejection of science. It's a conversation—an admittedly strange one—with an arachnid … a spider. And it's written for people like you, who may find themselves skeptical of grand claims, allergic to dogma, and more comfortable in a lecture hall or a lab than in a pew.

If you've ever rolled your eyes at theological certainty or squinted suspiciously at cosmic purpose, you're not alone. I spent much of my young adult life doing the same. And yet, somewhere between physics and philosophy, quantum weirdness, and moral intuition, I began to wonder: What if the truth isn't hiding *from* us … but *with* us? In the ordinary. In the overlooked. Even in something as absurd as a spider's web.

The conversation with the arachnid in these pages borders on fiction—but the questions do not. They're the ones whispered when no one's around. The ones Google can't quite satisfy. The ones that keep the clever and the curious off balance.

My goal isn't to convert you. It's to invite you into a web of thought, inquiry, wit, and maybe even wonder. And if, by the end, you feel a slight but unfamiliar tug in your heart, then that brief dialogue achieved its purpose.

Welcome to the conversation... and evidence in the web.

1

Bitten!

With additional time on my hands since my retirement, I was now able to do the many things I always wanted to do. One of those was exploring various walking trails throughout my area. Fortunately, the designers and planners of my fair state had the foresight to include lakes, parks, playgrounds, and campsites in their community developments so we could enjoy the many sights and sounds of nature that are found here. Given the variety of trail options at one of the parks I frequent, I decided one day to take a route I was familiar with. It was a short walk from my place to the park's trail, and I immediately headed down the steep grade to the paved pathway entering the woods. On this particular day, under the clear blue sky, a faint breeze in the air stirred up a fragrance I didn't quite recognize but welcomed as it pleasantly reminded me that this was a great day for observing nature while on a leisurely stroll.

It was early summer, but the heavy rains of spring had caused the vegetation to grow quickly and densely throughout the park, particularly on both sides of the trail. I passed through the entrance and headed along the path. The trees – maple, hickory, and birch – stood tall and scattered about on either side. The trees closest to the trail often canopied the path with their full overhanging branches. I suddenly realized that the fragrance I didn't recognize earlier was coming from the birch trees … a kind of wintergreen scent. The further I went, the path naturally narrowed, and the pavement eventually gave way to grass and then a mix of dirt and gravel. By now, the foliage had gotten quite dense, and on either side of the path, just a couple of feet away, spider webs among the vegetation were becoming more frequent.

The most common were the tangled webs or cobwebs of various sizes that covered much of the shrubbery. Close to the ground were the sheet webs with multiple layers of silk spread across patches of grass, with the spiders probably lurking somewhere under them. But the most eye-catching were the orb webs and the spiders that make them; they were predominant in size and the most intimidating. And having frequented this path many times, I was reminded that I was approaching a massive orb web.

Uncomfortably low overhead and situated between a couple of protruding tree branches, it was occupied by a long-legged orb-weaving spider that liked to position itself a little to the left, hovering just above passersby. Without even thinking, I automatically veered right, as I usually do, to avoid going directly under it. But suddenly, I felt a slight tug on the right side of my cap as if it was momentarily snagged on something.

Uh ho! I must have blundered into another spider's web, noticing thin strands of silk dangling from my jacket and cap. Then – PLOP! Something landed on my shoulder. And before I knew it, I felt a sharp pin prick on my neck. As I grabbed my neck, something scurried down my right side and the back of my leg.

I spun around to look, and a "large" long-legged orb weaver leaped from my leg to the ground and started scampering away. Stunned by the severity of the pain… and the size of the spider, I managed to yell out, "You BIT me?!"

To my shock, it stopped, turned, and yelled, "Yes, honey, I BIT you," using the word "honey" in a way that immediately reminded me of my late matronly aunt Esther, who, though quite nurturing at times, was also a no-nonsense disciplinarian, honed from her many years as a high school vice-principal.

"For what?" I blurted back, not fully grasping that she had spoken – let alone that I understood her.

"For what?! For what?!" she repeated angrily. "Because you carelessly…. no, STUPIDLY destroyed in a few seconds what took a whole night for me to construct! When you venture out here and mess with my masterpiece, that makes you my enemy … and there are consequences. You're too big to eat … so a good bite may teach you a lesson.

"I was trying to AVOID your web. I always do every time I walk past here. This is your first time building all the way over on this side of the path… and this low … I'm SORRY I wrecked your *webwork*."

She paused as though calculating something. Then I heard her mutter, "Let's see … two, three, four nights, but you … five days ago … oh my," apologetically looking at me. "You're right. You last came by five days ago, so you couldn't have known I'd expanded my empire. Now I'M embarrassed… for having bit you."

"Well, that's just great," I said, still covering the bite area with my hand, "but I'm probably poisoned now, thanks to you."

"Oh sugar," rolling several of its eyes (I assumed), "don't get your knickers in a twist. I may be venomous, but I'm not poisonous – at least not to you humans."

Still feeling a little hazy from the experience, I replied, "That's a relief," exhaling the breath I hadn't realized I was holding.

But then she added, "HOWEVER, let me put it this way, you won't DIE, but you MAY have a reaction."

She gave a little chuckle, which irritated me and also had me wondering what kind of "reaction" she was talking about.

Giving in to my irritation, I snapped "Next time put up a sign that says, 'CAUTION: MAJOR WEBWORK COMPLETED—AVOID AT ALL COSTS.'"

"I see you got jokes," she shot back. "Like I can make a sign with all those words on it. But I DO like that term … 'WEBWORK.' Maybe I'll spin that in: MAJOR WEBWORK—BEWARE!" she said, practically rolling on the ground, legs in the air, laughing.

2

Gettin' Schooled by an Arachnid

"It's not that funny," I grumbled. Then the realization hit me… I WAS TALKING TO A SPIDER! "Wait a minute – how am I even talking to a spider?"

"First of all, sugar," she said emphatically, "I am NOT a SPIDER. And second, you ought to be asking how you are HEARING and UNDERSTANDING what an *ARACHNID* – if you know Greek - is saying, or, if Latin is your preference … an *ARENEA.*"

"What are you talking about? You ARE a spider," I insisted, ignoring her references to ancient languages.

"No, I'm NOT," she objected.

"Yes, you ARE," I retorted.

"OK, honey, you're about to GET SCHOOLED!" She seemed quite confident in herself as she continued. "You humans have a habit of substituting the proper names of things with mundane ones to suit your lack of ability in navigating those names based on the age-old languages from which they were created, turning what was elegant into something common, making them simple for you to say and easy to remember, even when the substitution is incorrect."

"What do you mean?" I asked, not sure where this was going.

"Let's take the name COCCINELLIDAE, for example."

"The what?"

"The COC-CI-NELL-I-DAE," she repeated deliberately and slowly as if I was suffering from a learning disability. Then she paused, waiting for me to recognize the word. But seeing that I was clueless, she spurted out, "You humans call them *ladybugs*."

"Oh, ladybugs," I said, finally catching on. "So?"

With piercing looks from her eight eyes, she asked, "Well, you do realize they can't ALL be *ladies*, right?"

I hesitated, then shrugged. "Well, I guess I never really thought about it, but yeah, that makes sense."

"And why is that?" she pressed.

"Because, I guess there has to be some male ladybugs – ah er – 'manbugs' to mate with the females to make little Cocci … whatever," I replied, feeling a little ridiculous not being able to give a more intelligible answer.

"Very good!" she said, as though congratulating a child for finally doing something right. "They are Coccinellidae, and that's what they should be called. Tell me, honey, what's your name?"

"My given name is James."

She thought for a second. "Can I call you Jimmy?"

"Well, Jimmy was actually what I went by when I was a—"

"How about Jimmy Jam?" she interrupted. "Or Jimbo? Jamsie? Jam…"

"OK … OK!" I objected, louder than intended. "JAMES is proper and sufficient. I GET your point."

"Exactly. If your proper name is just fine for you, why isn't calling them Coccinellidae just fine as well? Why call them ladybugs when you know, and I know, and *everybody* knows they're not all ladies!"

As I was about to respond, it hit me again that I was talking to a spider – er, an *arachnid* (I preferred the Greek). "Wait, how is it you can speak my language?"

"Oh my goodness … my … goodness," she said, fanning herself with her many legs and feigning amazement. "You're asking *how* it is that I speak your language and not how I'm even speaking to you at all?"

"Look, I'm smarter than you think," I replied, bristling. "I'll have you know I'm a retired professor with three degrees."

"Say what?" she asked, apparently shocked.

"Yes, I have a doctorate and two master's," I said proudly.

She seemed to think for a moment. "What are your *degrees* in, baby?" she asked, emphasizing the word degrees with my aunt's sarcastic way of probing.

"I have a doctorate in international business, a master's in business, and a master's in engineering," rattling them off, trying to keep my chin up … exuding a little pride for my achievements.

"I seeeee," she said, dragging out the word. "So, you skipped engineering undergrad, did ya???"

I stared at her, realizing she somehow already knew the answer… that I had overlooked my undergrad degree in my count. "Uh, no, " I reluctantly admitted. "I got a bachelor's in engineering as well."

"Soooooo," she said with satisfaction, "if my count is correct, that's four degrees, not three. Right?"

"Uh, well… yes, but—"

"NO BUTS!" she scolded. "You have FOUR degrees, not three… for an engineering-international business EX-college professor, it seems your rudimentary math skills could use some polishing," and muttered something about the ridiculousness of an engineer with a doctorate that can't count to four. Then she sarcastically chided, "Tell you what, sugar … getting back to your question, I think I'd better *simplify* my answers just so you can understand them."

I started to protest her rebuke but given my track record with this arachnid thus far, I decided to stay quiet and listen.

"It's like this," she continued, "we arachnids have been around for eons, I've *molted* more times than you can count. Oops … sorry, that wasn't meant to be a joke. Anyway, species like mine are not wanderers; we're orb-weavers. Which means we intently search for and find a nice, productive spot, and we set up shop, so to speak, and stay there until the food source dries up – no pun intended."

She let off a little chuckle, then resumed. "That can be weeks, even months, unless some nincompoop" – giving me a pointed look – "comes along and destroys all our hard work in seconds. Then we must rebuild … or move on. And unless conditions at that location have changed to the extent that our survival is at risk, we will always rebuild, and will repeat that cycle over and over and over again because that's what we do to survive."

I nodded, purposely remaining quiet.

3

Engineering Marvels and Divine Design

"You see, honey, your background *includes* engineering, but the Creator wired us for engineering, architectural design, manufacturing, and even artistry.

"Wait a minute," I interrupted, "how do you figure you're able to do all that? I mean I can understand the design part … but engineering? Manufacturing? And artistry?"

"Well, sugar," she said matter-of-factly, "Be patient, and you'll learn what's what, 'cause your schooling isn't over! Let's see… where was I?" She wondered out loud. "Oh yeah, you see all this handiwork of mine … the web's design and structure?"

"Yes, of course."

"It's all developed to meet the specific purposes I deem necessary for my survival. For example, the primary orb structure's shape, size, and angles are determined based on such factors as what anchors are used, like a tree trunk or its branches, or leafy foliage. I have to take into account the existence and strengths of breezes or wind currents and their proximities and frequencies. I must also consider my size and weight, and that of my intended prey, and even potential predators. Moreover, there are sectional threads connecting the orb structure to its anchors – in my case, the tree trunk on that side, and over here, a branch of the tree on this side. These anchoring threads require varying strengths to secure the web's position and amply distribute the stress and vibrations from ongoing tremors and wind currents to the anchors I previously mentioned."

"Next, from the center of the orb and outward, strategically networked strands work as sensors, transmitting signals to inform me what type of disturbance is present. Whether it's nature's breezes causing the disturbance, a cautious male coming to mate, or a potential predator or prey, I will know what it is in an instant and what I need to do."

"And everything is intricately designed and formed to work together. I even use weather-resistant, biodegradable material, so that, as part of normal maintenance and rework, I can consume whatever is no longer useful and recycle it. You could say, sugar, I have a zero-waste policy and it's all Eco-friendly," she giggled.

"But I digress." She snapped. "You want to know how I learned to speak your language, right?"

"That's right," I sheepishly responded, hoping not to be the brunt of another admonishment.

She immediately resumed, "Since I've been perched above this path for so long, I've had the opportunity to hear the conversations of a whole lot of different humans passing by – running, walking, and even stopping to sit at that bench over there. Day after day, as I hung down from my web, I started listening carefully and began to pick up words and their meanings here and there. I also watched their behaviors and facial expressions as they talked, and some things began making sense. After a while – and I do mean a long, long while – I started to understand a little of their conversations, and then, a little more until I was getting pretty good at comprehending what they were saying."

"However, I then wanted to reason with them, particularly on the subjects of nature and the present surroundings, since on numerous occasions many of them lacked solid perspectives on these topics. But what to do, since I never tried talking before!?"

"And so, to answer the question you DIDN'T ask … How is it that I can talk? Well, I don't have vocal cords like you, but I can produce sounds by rubbing specialized parts of my body together, creating vibration patterns to form the words you hear. Although what you're hearing mimics the human voice, I am actually amplifying those patterns of vibrations and sounds through my body and out my *chelicerae* or mouth to reproduce the words."

"It took a lot of practice to develop that skill, and it consumes a lot of energy to produce these sounds at a volume level high enough for you to perceive them!"

"As a matter of fact," she added, "I hope you appreciate that I am expending a large amount of energy and time to school you on what's what."

"I assure you," answering in all honesty, "I do appreciate it."

"You see, honey," she continued, "If I'd located myself in some out-of-the-way undisturbed spot where no humans passed by, I'd be clueless as the day I hatched. But here, well, you could say, sugar, that fortune shined down on me."

"I guess that makes sense." After taking a few seconds to reflect on what she had just revealed, I asked. "So, after all that time listening and studying us, how well do you know our language, anyway?"

"That's a very good question," she replied. After thinking about it for a minute, she said, "If I had to guess, I'd say I know it well enough to pass a freshman English class in most of your colleges – maybe not all of them, mind you … but most of them."

I quietly chuckled.

"Go ahead, laugh," she said. "But I'm serious. If you haven't noticed, for one, I am a fan of what you humans call the "dead language" – Latin. This gives me a leg-up over most of you on learning your language, since generally speaking, you have no interest in it. Second, as you can imagine, there's a variety of educated souls that pass by every day, or stop to rest there, having conversations on an even greater variety of topics. Some even return repeatedly and are again discussing with others the same topics, which is good for me when I am in learning mode. However, given all that I've learned, certain words are still a mystery to me."

"What do you mean? Give me an example, maybe I can help clear it up for you," I said, now completely caught up in this conversation.

She hesitated for a moment as if carefully choosing what she was going to say next. "I've heard humans use this word when talking to their dogs, when talking to each other about food, and even when speaking about each other, which is sometimes preceded or followed by their lips touching and them holding hands and hugging, like it's something special. If two of us arachnids ever got that close, one would end up the other's meal, if you know what I mean."

"Well, what is the word?" I insisted.

4

The Question of LOVE

"The word is *love … what*'s this *love thing* all about? It seems to be used in so many different ways." She fixed her eyes on me, intently awaiting my response.

Her question surprised me. I had to take a moment to think about how to explain "the love thing" to an arachnid that can't relate to it.

"Well," I began, "just as he who you referred to as the Creator wired you to do those things you talked about for your survival, that same Creator we call God, who is God the Father, the Son, and the Holy Spirit – made us in their image, and wired us for love because GOD IS LOVE.[1] God made *love* essential to our survival, as those things you described earlier are to your survival, and without it, we really can't live, at least not in the way he intended us to live."

"Wait a minute, honey, let's back up a little ... it sounds like you have several creators, not one ... is that right?" she questioned.

"I can see where it might be confusing, hearing that for the first time, but no, I refer to only one God – the Creator – one essence who reveals himself to us humans in three unique persons."

"But why three? Wouldn't one do?" she asked. "After all, this is the Creator we're talking about, yes?"

"That's true, but I believe the three persons - each with a specific role to humankind - are the best way God could show his love for us by demonstrating how that same love exists and has existed among them since before the beginning."

"OK, honey ... correct me if I'm wrong, but it sounds like the three-person love has to be different from the love used for dogs and food and such, yes?"

"Yes, when the word *love* is used for pets and so on, it is not about survival but *emotions.* It's used to express an overwhelmingly satisfying mixture of feelings one experiences from the presence or actions of another, such as a series of pleasant feelings evoked from the taste, aroma, or fragrance of a particular food or meal, or for a pet that exceedingly pleases us, or a favorite vacation spot, or anything that causes a welling up of positive emotions that we can't compare to anything else and find it difficult to articulate. In fact, the use of the word has become commonplace because it's casually used so often about so many things."

"Oh yeah, sugar. I hear it all the time."

"But the love that is God's being is the love he wired into us, which is essential to our survival; it is not about some fleeting affection or conditional human emotion, but it's unwavering and because it's from God, it's eternal – it perpetuates its existence and ours on this earth. That love is patient and kind. Love is not jealous or boastful or proud or rude. It does not demand its own way. It is not irritable, and it keeps no record of being wronged. It does not rejoice about injustice but rejoices whenever the truth wins out. Love never gives up, never loses faith, is always hopeful, and endures through every circumstance.[2] That's the love God is: forgiving, redeeming, and transforming lives."

"So, let me see if I got this right, the word *love* that I hear so much, which seems to be used rather casually, has little to do with your survival, yes?"

"That's right."

"So, what about the three-person love that is the Creator… and wants you humans to be, how's that workin'?"

"Here's the thing," I continued, "because of his loving nature, along with wiring us with the God kind of love, God also gave us free will, letting us make choices, including whether to love or not."

"Wait a minute! Even though I'm just a little old arachnid," she said sarcastically, "I know what's essential to my survival, and I use every bit of what the Creator gave me to survive, every day and every night, no questions asked! But you're saying the Creator let you humans choose whether or not you want what he designed into you?! To me, that's a no brainer – how could you not choose 'love' if it is essential to your survival?"

"Well, that's the interesting thing about free will, it gives us options, and unfortunately, there are too many who choose to believe they have a better way to survive, and they can survive without it, that is, without God's love, and even without God," I lamented.

"Now, baby, that would be hilarious if it wasn't so sad – the 'created' have better survival plans than their Creator and can do without the Creator in their lives."

"That's not the worst of it. There was a point very early on in the life of humankind where God wanted to make it clear that our choices mattered. He said, 'Today, I have given you the choice between life and death, between blessings and curses. Now I call upon heaven and earth to witness the choice you make. Oh, that you would choose life so that you and your descendants might live! You can make this choice by loving the Lord your God, obeying him, and committing yourself firmly to him. This is the key to your life … '[3] He couldn't have made it clearer, even pointing out which choice to make, for us and our descendants to survive."

"And I take it, honey, that the choice for life was not unanimous!" She paused for a minute, I assumed to reflect on this surprising revelation, and then said, "Well, hey, that's good news for the rest of creation, right?"

"How's that?" I asked, a little perplexed by her conclusion.

"Honey, please, there is no way the 'created' can out-think, out-design, out-plan, or out-do the Creator in any way, shape, or form. Even my arachnid babies, bless their hearts, have enough sense to know that. And since that's the case, we arachnids only need to sit back and let you humans destroy yourselves with those ridiculous notions and plans. We are easily going to out-survive you humans – it's just a matter of time," she concluded with rather unsettling yet persuasive reasoning.

"That's a bit simplistic, however—" I started to respond, but she interrupted me.

"Look, it is what it is," she said, shrugging a few legs, "I've wasted enough time schooling you on what's what, although admittedly, I have a better understanding of the love thing now, but thanks to you, I also have a lot of re-work to do."

5

The Web of Silk

I realized she was about to turn and leave, and I knew that to convince her to stay, I needed to appeal to her penchant to 'school me,' so I pleaded, "Wait, you told me how you're wired to do architectural engineering, but the manufacturing part, how is that possible?!" That got her attention.

She turned around and looked straight at me acknowledging, "Oh, yeah, you're right," she shrugged, and immediately gathered herself, preparing to expound on an especially unique skill she had nearly overlooked.

"The fact is, sugar, of all the design and development capabilities the Creator gave me, the manufacturer in me is the most dynamic. It's like this, you could say I manufacture my own materials!" She paused and stared at me momentarily to again let what she just said sink in.

"Yeah, well, I didn't figure you imported them from China," I said, trying to make a joke, which she completely ignored.

"You see, I'm a silk specialization machine!"

"What do you mean?"

Cupping her lower body part with a couple of pairs of her legs, she resumed, "Inside my *opisthosoma* – my abdomen, in case you're wondering – is a system of gland-duct silk producing assemblages. They allow me to *custom-blend* my silk. Drawing from a unique assortment of selected proteins and by varying the speed at which I pull them through my silk ducts, I can make a variety of silk threads, each with its characteristic mechanical, structural, and functional properties."

"Wait!" I interrupted. "Just so I understand, you produce a variety of proteins that, in various combinations, let you make different types of silk threads?"

"That's right, honey!" "The mixture varies based on how I intend to use the silk fibers. For example, the primary orb structure you see there requires 18 of those proteins to form the strongest silk, which has a distinctive blend of strength and stretch-ability since, without tearing, it has to absorb the driving force from flying prey."

"Yes, I think I remember about that particular silk thread in school, is it called *major ampullate silk?"*

"That's right, sugar!

"You may not know how valuable that silk is to us humans. For years we used it as cross-hair for surveyors' telescopes and other optical devices. And it's been found to be three times stronger than Kevlar – the material used for bulletproof vests!"

"Well, I wouldn't know about all that, but what I do know is that it will stop and hold my prey just long enough for me to start meal prepping it!"

"Yes, I'd expect that it would." I said, truly fascinated. "But how do you know what strength is needed in the first place?"

"Adaptation, honey, adaptation. My web is always carefully designed according to strict parameters – its positioning, structure, and the strengths of its parts – are driven by the information I compile from the surrounding environment, combined with the need for efficiency. I maximize my capture probability without overextending the use of my materials or energy. But if my captured prey turns out to be larger or smaller than expected, I make the necessary modifications to my web parts, such as its size, spiral spacing, strength, and so on."

"Speaking of your prey," I wondered, "do you use some kind of glue on your web to make it sticky?"

"Oh, you know it, baby, for that, you might consider me a biochemical engineering wonder as well," she boasted, "I make a glue-like substance that I apply as microscopic deposits when I'm extruding the silk for the capture spiral, but it's not a liquid like the glue you humans use; it's an entanglement of cross-linked substrates working together that make them quite elastic and sticky. And if I may add, one of the deposits' properties includes the absorption of moisture from the air to retain its stickiness."

"Oh, wait a minute, I think that's called hygroscopic."

"Called what?" She wondered out loud.

"HY-GRO-SCO-PIC!" I replied, slowly pronouncing the syllables, taking the opportunity to teach her something again for a change. "Many of our everyday food products are hygroscopic, like table salt and sugar, but so are materials like nylon and wool."

"Whatever, anyway, it eliminates the need for me to keep replacing them as they start to lose their stickiness. How efficient is that!?" she noted, dismissing my attempt to school her for a change.

I could tell by her not-so-subtle boasts that she was enjoying the opportunity to enlighten me on "what's what" in her arachnid world.

She continued, "However, while I have waxed on about my stronger and stickier silks, at the other end of the spectrum, there's a silk I make, so delicate and light that my little ones use it to travel long distances on wind currents, ballooning here and there, with some traveling great distances to live in new locations."

"Uhhh, that's not something I want to imagine – hundreds of baby arachnids floating about in the air, landing on who knows what or who."

"Oh, don't worry, sugar, they are so tiny, ten of them could light on your bald head and you would never know," she laughed.

"That doesn't make me feel any better," I bristled, the hair standing up on the back of my sore neck.

"A-n-y-way, I expect you now understand why I claim that the Creator made me an architectural-biochemical engineering and manufacturing wonder," she finished, with an obvious attitude of satisfaction.

"OK, I give you that, and I appreciate all the details," I said, trying to stroke her ego to keep the conversation going. "But what's interesting is that you give the Creator all the credit for what you can do. If only we humans would give God credit in the same way for all the abilities he's gifted us. Even though we're made in his image, so many of us do not see his hand in our design or survival, or we refuse to see it."

"Sugar, you got that right!" she agreed, "My whole being understands that and operates ceaselessly with that understanding. Ya know, it's like you said, hardwired in, honey, hardwired in!"

"The sad thing is," I continued, "while God's handiwork in creating us along with the rest of the universe was declared thousands of years ago in ancient writings from which I quoted earlier, called the Scriptures, in more recent times, the existence of his design for our survival is being confirmed repeatedly through the one discipline that so many of these same people put all their faith in and yet even then … remain skeptical."

6

Quantum Physics and the Ultimate Observer

"Now that's hard to believe, Honey! What discipline are you talking about?" she asked.

"Science!" I replied.

She paused for a minute, processing what I said. "Wait … a … minute!" she shouted. "First, you tell me these humans believe they have a better survival plan than their Creator, and now, you're telling me the very thing they have put their trust in all along, is even validating God's design for their survival, and they don't believe IT either?!"

"Pretty much," I said, "otherwise, they would accept that he exists and his design for them. Instead, they remain skeptical for one reason or another."

"I'm sorry, honey, but there has GOT to be more to this than you're letting on," she insisted, "'cause this just doesn't make any sense at all to this arachnid!" she said, wringing her head with a few of her legs.

"Well, remember, having free will can work *for* us or *against* us depending on the choices we make, and that's exactly what scientists are finding out today through their research and experiments."

"Hold up, I'm guessing, but hasn't science been around for a long time?"

"I see where you are going with the question, and yes, it has. But as one theoretical physicist noted years ago, "Science advances one funeral at a time,"[4] and God will allow anyone, particularly scientists, the opportunity to prove or disprove his existence, during their lifetime. However, to any scientist who honestly applies his knowledge, skills, and understanding in determining God's existence, God will reveal himself to that person."

"But how do you know that?" she asked.

"Well, remember those ancient writings I referred to earlier, the Scriptures, in them God said so, that "If you look for me wholeheartedly, you will find me" for his intent was always that we seek him and find him, even though he is not far from any one of us.[5] And with respect to science, the Scriptures also say 'The heavens proclaim the glory of God. The skies display his craftsmanship. Day after day they continue to speak; night after night they make him known. They speak without a sound or word; their voice is never heard. Yet their message has gone throughout the earth, and their words to all the world…,' and again, 'They know the truth about God because he has made it obvious to them. For ever since the world was created, people have seen the earth and sky. Through everything God made, they can clearly see his invisible qualities - his eternal power and divine nature. So they have no excuse for not knowing God.'"[6]

"It's a crying shame, honey, that they don't see what's in front of their faces!"

"Or, maybe they don't want to see it," I remarked. "But this is where it gets really interesting – where the 'rubber meets the road' you might say."

"Where the what meets the what?"

"Never mind … I'm just saying that since the beginning of creation, while God has revealed himself to us in so many ways through the naked eye, in more recent times, through advances in science and technology, God is also giving us glimpses of himself, where the naked eye can't see. And in this case, he is doing so through the most fundamental of all sciences called *quantum physics*."

"Quantum physics? Baby, that sounds deep. Are you going to break it down for this arachnid?"

"Certainly! I'm glad you asked. Quantum physics is the study of matter and energy at the most elementary level – waves and atomic and subatomic particles. Quantum physicists seek to discover the properties and behaviors of the building blocks of life."

"That sounds like creation stuff, so they're delving into the Creator's arena, yes?"

"Yes, and as He promised … He will reveal himself to anyone who seeks him with all his heart, but…"

"But, what?" "But, he also promises to show his anger to those who, by their wickedness, prevent the truth from being known."[7]

"I don't understand – why wouldn't a person of science, whose profession, I expect, is to seek the truth, not make the truth known once it's discovered?!"

"First of all, that can happen due to human error. Scientists are human and when it comes to performing research or solving problems, they can make honest mistakes in their efforts to seek the truth. I experienced that many times in my profession while trying unsuccessfully to solve an engineering or physics problem, unaware of an error I had made in my assumptions or what was missing from my argument, preventing me from getting the correct answer."

"Yes, sugar, I can believe that," she chuckled, taking another jab at me.

"But," resuming my point, "I was always open to being corrected and accepting what was determined to be the correct answer and approach to solving the problem. Unfortunately, some have accomplished a level of achievement and influence, and then use their influence to obscure or cover up what they know to be true because that truth may conflict with their worldview, their values, their love of money or power, or for whatever reason. That's what God refers to as *wickedness*, stating 'They exchanged the truth about God for a lie, and worshiped and served created things rather than the Creator …'[8] They know the truth, but intentionally prevent the truth from being known to others."

"So, are you saying this science called quantum physics conflicts with some scientists' values, worldviews, or the desire for other things?" she asked.

"My answer is yes, in many cases. You see, the properties by which things function or operate at the quantum level break from the traditional Newtonian physics that you and I rely on every day as we navigate our respective worlds."

"Oh? So, when I determine the strength needed by my capture web to overcome the driving force of my potential prey flying into it, I am using 'Newtonian physics,' as you call it?"

"Yeah. You're using Newton's laws of motion, particularly the ones regarding equal and opposite forces and the kinetic energy of your prey. The difference between you and us humans is that these laws are designed into you – you know and apply them automatically, whereas we must *learn* them."

"And I bet some learn quicker than others, yes?!" She smirked, having fun throwing a taunt at me again.

"Nevertheless!" I continued, "The fact is, these laws are invalidated at the quantum level!"

"How so?" she said, showing a genuine interest.

"Well, for example, when objects travel at the speed of light, Newton's laws of motion do not hold, or when dealing with sub-atomic elements, those laws do not apply. Both are natural phenomena found in the quantum realm."

"OK. So, if this quantum stuff is so fundamental, what is there not to believe about it?"

"That's what's so funny. It's not about the validity of the science – it can't be refuted; it's more regarding the questions it's raising about how we came to be: *How* we were created and *who* created us that challenges the thinking of those who repudiate, with vigor I might add, God's existence and us as his handiwork! It's as if, through quantum physics, God is allowing us glimpses of his existence and his part in our creation, but they refuse to see it."

"Interesting, what kind of glimpses?"

"Well, first, the principles of quantum physics alter our view of how things operate in our world. Moving us from Newton's deterministic model, which has been around for centuries and fundamentally influential in how we perceive *reality*, to a probabilistic mode, challenging that perception."

"And it does this, how?"

"The Newtonian model, with its predictable realities fixed in space and time, has been the foundation of engineering and modern technology for centuries, and even treats humans deterministically as machines with exchangeable parts. Now, enter quantum physics, which informs us that the building blocks of all matter embrace uncertainty. For example, particles can exist as waves and waves as particles, which is known as *wave-particle duality*.[9] A particle can also exist in multiple states simultaneously, called *superposition*; it remains in a state of uncertainty until we observe it, which causes it to change its behavior, referred to as the *observer effect*.[10]

"Like I said, honey, sounds like the Creator's arena."

"And lastly, they can affect each other instantaneously regardless of the distance between them; that's called *entanglement*. So, you can see how these revelations upended the Newtonian model with its fixed realities, such that reality, at its most fundamental level, is anything but deterministic. In fact, you could say it's *in-deterministic*."

"Well, sugar, what I see is that you've got two models here between which there is an unexplained gap, yes?"

"Yes, that's about right, but if those same humans weren't so set on dismissing the idea that God does indeed exist and is the Creator of all that was made, I believe that 'gap,' as you call it, would be resolved sooner rather than later, if ever. For example, the observer effect says that a given subatomic element exists in superposition except when we observe it, and the very act of our observing it collapses it into a locatable object."

"OK, I follow that, but what does that have to do with—"

"Look, quantum physics tells me this walking stick I'm using, of physical matter, is comprised of subatomic building blocks that, by my conscious observation, have collapsed into a walking stick. It is visible as a walking stick – I see it as a walking stick."

"OK, but how does that relate to the Creator—"

"Let me ask you this: if, by my conscious observation, I'm collapsing subatomic elements to create the reality around me, what or who collapsed me into this reality, from my fundamental building blocks, which are far more complex than this walking stick?"

There was silence as she considered the question, scratching her head with a couple of her legs while her eyes wandered in every direction, trying to resolve this dilemma.

And then, as if struck by lightning, the arachnid leaped into the air shouting, "The Creatorrrrrrr. The Creator is the *Ultimate Observer*!"

"I would say so. With all of our wonderfully complex anatomy, which he created, he collapsed us image-bearers into this dimension and gifted us, among other things, the ability to do our own *collapsing* … to create our own realities. But that's not all. The law of entanglement shows us that everything in time and space is relationship-driven, independent of distance and without need of a physical connection."

"Explain," she insisted.

"This interconnectedness facilitates the exchange of information between quantum elements instantaneously – some say, faster even than the speed of light."

"You don't say!"

“I do say, but there’s more. In the field of neurobiology—”

“Wait … what?!!”

“Neurobiology … a branch of biology that focuses on the makeup of our nervous system, including the study of our brain. It’s the discipline where mirror neurons were discovered about 30 years ago. They were found to be contributors to our connecting with each other on a deeper level. I believe that God meant for us to live via those interconnections, which is why he instituted prayer and told us to be persistent in it for one another.[11] When aligned with him, prayer is a way of impacting others’ lives, as well as our own. So, though the law of entanglement is characteristic of the fundamental building blocks of life, it also facilitates the interconnection between you and me and everyone else at the macro-cosmic level, sharing a common reality. As one neuroscientist put it, ‘Everything and everyone is linked, and we all affect each other.’”[12]

7

The Fall and Its Cosmic Consequences

"Well, even if what you are telling me is true, and I believe it is, it's not that easy to get my head around it all, even for this sharp-as-a-thorn arachnid."

"The term, for your information, is 'sharp-as-a-TACK," I said, taking an opportunity to correct her for a change.

But she retorted, "Not from where I sit, honey. How many tacks do you see around here? However, there are a lot of thorns in my world, and if you ever got stuck by one, you'd remember it. But as I was saying, though you seem to have a pretty good handle on all this stuff, I would guess that most of you humans don't understand it well enough to even be interested, let alone relate it to the Creator as his handiwork. I'm surprised he didn't use a simpler approach to inform you all of his existence and plan for your lives."

"He did. Here again it's written in the Scriptures, going back over several thousand years."

"Seriously?"

"Yep! The Scriptures were another of his gifts to humankind, telling us His story and how to live the way He created us to live. Those of us who believed them call them the Holy Bible or Bible because God, who inspired it, is Holy and complete and everything he does is holy or complete."

"And what do those who don't believe what it says, call it?" she wryly asked.

"As you can imagine, some things that aren't too flattering, although I have to admit that throughout the history of us believers, as messengers touting it as God's Word, we could have done a better job of sharing its truths. Too often, I think, we used it as the hammer of God, trying to pound it into people rather than sharing it as his instructional love letter of life from him to us and for us."

"So, you're saying that in this Bible you're talking about, the Creator explained all this quantum stuff in a way that most would understand?"

"In a manner of speaking, yes, it was written for the benefit of all generations, so those hearing his words for the first time, even back then, were able to perceive what he was saying in the context they could understand."

"Meaning he had to use words they could relate to in their particular space and time."

"Correct."

"Well, that makes sense."

"Yeah, and although it took about 1,500 years to complete these writings by more than 60 different writers and was made available in its final form only about six hundred years ago. If we read it carefully, even today … while examining our own hearts … the message would be clear: God's sole desire was and is to have a personal relationship with us."

"Remember when I explained that God is love and defined it the way I did?"

"Oh yeah, honey, that's the one takeaway I won't forget!"

"Well, those exact words are found in this Bible."

"What about all that neurobiological stuff you talked about?"

"That too … for example, about 2,000 years ago, he told us 'As a man thinks in his heart, so is he.'"[13]

"The Creator said that way back then? Ohhhh, that's good, sugar," she remarked, beginning to connect the dots. "Even though I'm not human, I can relate. Once I've found a location for my web, somehow I know exactly what to do and how, taking into account all those things I mentioned, like anchor stresses, wind factors, silk placements and strengths, design, size, et cetera, et cetera, and I make it happen. It all comes together just as I see it within me. That kinda mimics the concept that a human becomes what he thinks about, yes?"

"It's similar. What a man thinks in his heart, shapes his beliefs and defines his behaviors, but in your case, it's a little different; you're hardwired to do what you do, so you do it automatically, or you won't survive. Since we have free will, we weigh our options before we make a decision, and even then, we can change our minds if we choose.

"Change your minds? Sounds like that could be confusing, let alone detrimental to your survival."

"Indeed!" I added. "Down through the ages, at national

levels, taking opposite sides or switching sides on an important issue have been the causes for wars; at the level of commerce and industry, it has filled courts with countless legal battles, and, sadly, at the societal level, it has been the source of many irate, and even violent, disagreements resulting in broken relationships – and worse."

"Nevertheless, this observer effect, not to mention other intricately designed workings of our mind-brain-body inter-connections also inform us of a creative consciousness far greater than our own, which has created us like itself to be "entangled" with itself – transcending space and time – so that we may be connected to that consciousness, fellow-shipping with him and thereby be instructed, encouraged, and guided to actualize his purpose of love, peace, and order for us in this world. This is why I said earlier that God wired us for love! This means our minds, brains, and bodies were designed to think, choose, and act according to that internal design, reflecting his will and purpose for us. But rather than *forcing* us to live by his design, he gave us the right to choose, knowing he was risking rejection in the process."

"Honey, the Creator is the master of it all, so I know he knew the odds before he even started."

"Oh, no doubt, and unfortunately, rejection wasn't long in coming," I lamented. "It occurred through the disobedience by the first of us humans, and the consequences of that rebellion were catastrophic – for them and all humans after them, and even for the rest of creation!

"That doesn't sound good, sugar! What happened?"

"First, the law of entanglement was altered between his consciousness and ours; he could not have the relationship with us he had in the beginning. Moreover, our consciences, due to our rejection of him, were now vulnerable to other influences – forces bent on chaos and destruction."

"Hmmmm, sounds like you all invited some serious trouble for yourselves as well as the rest of us," she commented, sounding a little agitated.

"Yes, but the good news is God never gave up on us or his hope for us, and just as you might expect, his plan already in place, included that two-edged sword called our free will that by it, in time, we would come to desire the relationship with him he always wanted, helping to restore it, regenerating that conscious connectedness, as it was originally intended."

"Well, how's that workin', cause from where I sit it seems like you all have a penchant for changing your minds, and it usually results in confusion and strife – not love, not peace, and certainly not the *order* you speak of."

"I might have painted for you a darker picture than intended. Throughout the ages, there were also some bright spots, despite our rebellion. Many sought to know God, and some became his messengers; through them he continued to show His character to us and remind us of His goodwill and purpose for us – and it is through them he chose to record His story, from beginning to end."

"Well, honey, that should've settled it. With the Creator's story in hand so that you know what's what, everyone should be going with the flowing, yes?"

"It's go with the flow, and that's true, but—"

She interrupted again, "Don't tell me, you're going to start talking about free will again."

"Yep, and the fact that our consciousness, now lacking that initial relationship with his, left us with having to deal with those malevolent forces I mentioned earlier – forces bent on our destruction, which, from that time until now, have been at work, from age to age, and generation to generation, throughout the world."

"You know, with all that intelligence you humans claim to have, choosing your own survival paths and such over the Creator's, seems like you would have solved that problem by now, yes!?"

"Well, until we are willing to swallow our pride and admit that we're not that smart, then no, that problem will not get solved. As an example, some propose to solve the problem by denying that God exists, or they disparage the validity of the Scriptures, or make other unproven propositions and statements. Look, pride has been a problem with us since the beginning when the first of God's creation looked at himself and let his glorious beauty go to his head and declared he was going to become greater than God himself."

"No way! Not another human trying to do his own thing, too?"

"Oh no … God's first creation, called Lucifer, wasn't human, he was an angel –

in fact, the highest ranking among all the guardian angels God had created, and is said to have been perfect until his excessive love for his own beauty and splendor filled him with pride and corrupted his wisdom"[14]

"*Corrupted* his wisdom? Corrupted his wisdom? What's that mean? Did he go crazy or something?!"

"That's an interesting way of putting it," I laughed, "but yeah, you could say anyone or anything that thinks it's going to make itself greater than the God who created it must be crazy, right? And as a result, he was expeditiously removed from heaven and hurled to earth along with about a third of all the angels that remained loyal to him. You might say it was the first mass exodus of record," I added, attempting to interject some humor.

Ignoring my comment, the arachnid looked rather pensive for a moment, "Hmmmm, hurled to earth." Then she asked whimsically, "So maybe that's how you humans got the idea of doing your own thing, perhaps listening to this crazy Lucifer?"

"You know," I remarked, "it's amazing how you can put two and two together so quickly."

"Sharp as a thorn, sugar, I'm telling you, sharp as a thorn!"

"Well, you're right, but having lost his position in heaven, he was no longer called Lucifer, but was given a new name, Satan, meaning 'adversary,' and later, the devil, meaning 'accuser,' denoting his new position and role relative to humankind.

"Uh oh," she remarked, "that doesn't sound too good for you all."

"Once again, you're correct. Satan set his sights on the two humans God created, named Adam and Eve, and immediately went to work using his deceptive means, causing them to rebel against God, and thereby usurping their authority – the authority God had given to them. These two are who I was talking about earlier, and this is why I said it was catastrophic, placing all of creation under a cursed being, making us cursed as well."

"Oh now, I see what you mean honey – they didn't just disobey the Creator, they did so by obeying that crazy angel, Satan, yielding to him the authority they had been given by the Creator. But they couldn't have known what they were doing, could they?"

"Well, perhaps not totally. They were fresh on the scene, so I doubt if they knew the full ramifications of what they were doing or had done, but Adam knew he was disobeying

God's command when he did what he did, and so he was held responsible for what transpired: all creation-the earth and everything in it-becomes corrupted or cursed under this new corrupt authority, missing the mark of what God originally intended. This also meant that since Adam's and Eve's bodies were made from the earth, their bodies, and all born after them, were to suffer that same corruption or missing of the mark, which is called *sin.*"

"Sin," she noted out loud, and looking pensive again, she asked, "Missing the mark of what?"

"Missing the mark of God's love and all the benefits that go with it – that's all sin is, pure and simple. The sad thing about Adam and Eve's situation is that for the rest of their lives, they had to carry the memory of how it used to be, that is, the relationship they had with God before they disobeyed him.

"Oh, honey, that's harsh – it seems that would be punishment enough along with having to deal with that crazy angel, but what I don't get is why the Creator let it go that far. If it was me, I would've nipped it all in the bud from the jump, you know what I mean?"

"He did! I believe when Lucifer said he was going to become greater than God, in effect, God said, 'No you won't,' which immediately settled it and set into motion the events I just described, and all subsequent events to completely fulfill God's response."

"So here we are."

8

The Plan for Redemption

"Yes, here we are, and nothing has changed in the sense that we're still dealing with that age-old curse, on the earth and, for many, in ourselves, while having to make choices every day. But neither has God changed… despite the naysayers, he continues to show us his loving character in many different ways and to invite us to have a personal relationship with him."

"Well, honey, I believe it. You said love never gives up, right? But how is that ever going to be possible since – and I am assuming this – that crazy angel isn't likely to give up that authority it stole?"

"I'm glad you asked, because about 2,000 years ago in fact,

God 'put some skin in the game,' as it were, and clothed his son in a human form to come down to earth to live with us so that we might see him in action, that is, how to live according to his will and purpose in this hostile and corrupted environment. His plan not only included living among us as one of us, but it also included Him dying for us and then returning to his heavenly home once he took back that authority from Satan."

"Wha-wait, what?! Honey I know you're not saying the Creator is dead, and why would he want to die for you all anyway. From what you've been telling me, none of you humans even deserve that kind of consideration?"

"Let me finish, OK? You're exactly right, but remember, when I said Adam was held accountable and judged for putting us in this cursed situation?"

"I remember!"

"Well, bear in mind that Adam started out, created by God, without a human father, free of that sin nature, living under the perfect law of entanglement until he chose to disobey God. So afterward, now cursed, Adam passed that same judgment on to all his descendants, us, so that each was burdened with that same sin nature, being separated from God's consciousness, which ultimately results in death."

"That makes sense – the Creator, being Holy or complete, can't be entangled with anyone who has missed the mark, as it were," she noted in all seriousness.

"And since God knew that no man, born of a natural father, could fix this situation due to their cursed nature, He sent the perfect man, His Son, at the perfect time to fix it himself. So, the Son came and took on a curse-less human form – just like Adam had initially, effectively making him the second Adam – and took a human name, Jesus, which means 'God is salvation,' and He lived among us for more than 30 years, being the perfect model for us to live by and never making Adam's mistake of disobedience."

"But you said the Creator died, and that's not possible since he's the Creator!"

"Keep in mind that to undo this curse on humankind, the second Adam, Jesus, had to nullify what was done by the first Adam. When the first Adam disobeyed God, Adam and all his descendants by natural birth suffered the consequences of missing the mark, death, that's the price that had to be paid. However, the second Adam, after living in obedience to God's will and purpose all his life, never missing the mark, could then *voluntarily* die to pay the price for all of us, as only He could."

"So, is the Creator dead?"

"Not at all, His mortal body died, paying the price we would've all had to pay, but He wasn't finished. He still wanted us to have that relationship with Him the first Adam had initially, so Jesus was raised from the dead in a new resurrected body. Therefore, while all humankind died through the first Adam, all will be made alive, that is, resurrected, through the second Adam, Jesus, if only we believe in Him and accept Him as our LORD and Savior."

"Uh huh, honey, that's my Creator for ya … he leaves no stone unturned!"

"That's not all, in the process of all this, since the price was now paid, Jesus took back the authority Satan had usurped from the first Adam and made a show of Satan's defeat for all the angels to see. Jesus even told His disciples after His resurrection that 'I have been given all authority in heaven and on earth.'"[15]

"Phew! You had me going there, sugar! Now I just feel like dancing … the Creator won BIG TIME," she shouted as she began moving her legs in a rhythmic motion and bouncing up and down as if doing some arachnid dance ritual.

"Yes, Jesus won big time, and WE won big time because of what He did! And what He did has had such an impact on humankind, today, nearly 50% of the world's human population celebrates His earthly birthday every year … we call it Christmas."

"Oh, my goodness, that would have been something to see and experience … the Creator right down here with me …" she imagined out loud as she seemed to run out of gas from all the dancing around.

"Yet, despite all that, many still reject who He is and what he did. On the other hand, there were also many who received him as their Lord – that is, believed in who He is and what He did. Therefore, returning to my original premise, the most fundamental of all sciences, quantum physics has been giving us glimpses of God's existence and us as his handwork, and yet many of those who have trusted in science most of their lives, are finding reasons to not believe what science is inferring when it comes to God's existence."

"Baby, it seems there will always be those who have a reason for rejecting the Creator … yes!?"

"You may be right, but my hope – and I'm sure His also – is that many more will come to accept Him, believe in Him, and embrace the relationship He offers, before their time runs out."

"Well, honey, speaking of time," she said, already crawling away. "Mine has run out and I've got too much work to do – again, thanks to you. No more questions!"

"Wait!" I hollered. She stopped in her tracks, turned, and looked inquiringly at me. I asked, "But what about the 'artist thing' you mentioned?" I had to dangle a metaphorical carrot

… or rather … fly, in front of her to get her attention back since I wasn't finished.

"Ohhhh…" she said, letting out a long breath of frustration, "OK, but this is it!"

And she went on to explain, "While I could wax poetically about my ah … what did you call it… 'webwork,' it wouldn't be far from the truth to say that you may have even seen my orb designs at art shows or in galleries. I remember a couple of occasions when people stopped here or there where you're standing and with professional-looking cameras and other equipment, positioned themselves in front of me and started taking a lot of pictures of me and my workmanship."

"You know, I remember attending a couple of art shows in my time where there were displays of interesting photos of spider … er ah, arachnid' webs of various species. Of course, no telling whether or not they were photos of your web."

"I wish I could have seen them, sugar, I would have known right away if they were mine. Nevertheless, although I must admit that while I am pretty good at web working, there is another of my species, my cousin the *Cyclosa*, that, because of her very small size, needs an edge to ward off potential predators. As such, she goes so far as to design and build a giant decoy arachnid in the middle of her orb web."

"So, she forms this decoy out of the silk she produces … in the same way you do?"

"Yes, in part, but she also uses small pieces of debris, dead insects, leaf fragments, and such, to add color and volume to the decoy's body and tentacles she formed that extend in every direction. But her *magnum opus*, honey, to make this creation appear real, she employs a pattern of pulses on specific silk threads that make it come alive to the eyes of a potential predator. It's so big, it naturally attracts the attention of the predators to it instead of to my small cous'. Even small birds that might otherwise consider her as potential prey are deterred because of the decoy's size, scary look, and life-like movements.[16]

"Like having her own puppet scarecrow," I said, laughing.

"Exactly! Not only is that art at its finest, but it's also the *ultimate* survival mechanism. So, there you are. The Creator has equipped us with whatever we need to survive, and unlike you humans, we all make good use of what he has given us... now that's it and no more! Goood-bye!" She shouted, then, swiftly spun around and disappeared under the leaves.

As I stood there, stunned a bit by her abrupt departure, an uncomfortable feeling crept upon me of suddenly being left alone on the trail of which I had made little progress, and so did the dreaded awareness of the stinging sensation in my neck. I hoped she was right about not being poisonous. As I tried to continue my walk, my head was spinning, wondering if this conversation really happened – or if it was some kind of hallucination from the bite – that "reaction" she spoke of.

I went home to rest, recover, and reflect on my very unusual encounter with a talking arachnid. I promised myself I would return after a few days to see the fully restored web she seemed so obligated to finish, and more importantly, continue my conversation with this unique arachnid that reminded me of my aunt Esther.

Four days passed, and I was as good as new; there was hardly even a trace of the bite mark, and the pain had long since left me. It was a weather-perfect day: warm sunshine, a light breeze, and none of the heavy winds like the previous few days. I rushed to the park trail and down the steep grade, excited to see my talking arachnid and her reconstructed masterpiece.

As I approached the spot on the path, looking up … my heart sank. The web was in total disrepair as if the previous day's winds had torn right through it, leaving only remnant strands of silk flowing in the breezes … and the arachnid was nowhere to be found.

"Maybe I DID imagine it all," I thought out loud, when suddenly I heard a gruff elderly male voice call out, "Hey, young fella! Are you that engineering professor I heard about with the math disability?"

I looked up to see a much smaller, all black and fuzzy-legged arachnid, clinging to the trunk of a tree where the orb web used to be.

"Come over here, sonny," it demanded, waving a leg at me, "so I can tell you what's what."

9

EPILOGUE

This unusual conversation is based on a real encounter I had with a large arachnid along a walking trail. Its orb web, at one point, did in fact, transverse the path not too high above my head, and from which it seemed content just to hang down. So, you couldn't pass by without noticing this long-legged creature dangling just above your head. I stared at it, and I'm sure it was staring back at me. I even had to take a couple of pictures with my cellphone. Did it talk to me? Well, I can tell you for sure, it didn't bite me.

However, shortly after that walk, I awoke around 2 in the morning, and the dialogue between the professor and the arachnid just began to flow through my mind. And I was reminded of the scripture in Rom. 8:19-22, which says, "For all creation is waiting eagerly for that future day when God will reveal who his children really are. **Against its will** (bold emphasis added), all creation was subjected to God's curse. But with eager hope, the creation looks forward to the day when it will join God's children in glorious freedom from death and decay. For we know that all creation has been groaning as in the pains of childbirth right up to the present time (NLT)."

The implication of these passages is most profound as they suggest the interconnection between creation's restoration and human redemption – the hope of believers' ultimate glorification and creation's anticipated liberation from decomposition, corruption, and futility. But more importantly, it made me realize that creation recognizes its broken and deteriorating state and continually longs for what once was in the beginning. Just like Adam and Eve after their rebellion, who for the rest of their lives could only reminisce and long for the days when they and God were together in the Garden, creation also remembers that idyllic time of its existence … and longs for its return as well. However, unlike creation and its confidence in God's existence and in His role in assuring its hope for the future, mankind, in general, remains irresolute – hiding from God and/or blaming him for its predicament, or worse, claiming that He doesn't even exist.

So, this brief rendition of a conversation between creation (the arachnid) and mankind (the professor) has a couple of purposes. To inform the reader: a) despite our repeated attempts to make life better, at the exclusion of God in our lives, things have only gotten worse and will continue to do so, b) that God does indeed exist and has continually revealed

Himself to us since the beginning of the ages, and c) anyone can come to know God and be made right with Him … no longer missing the mark of his love for them. Let me explain.

But first, the obvious. You've no doubt noticed the conversation between the arachnid and the professor is couched in a Christian framework. That's because I am a Christian, and the only perspective I could rightly present in this conversation is my own, from my knowledge and experiences. This means, then, I believe the Bible is the inspired Word of God – His instructional love letter to us, if you will, and as such I often use its truths, in addition to some academic and scientific materials, as support for the professor's points of view.

That said, regarding the first point, I'm reminded of one of the most committed persecutors of the early Christian church, Saul of Tarsus, and his first encounter with the Lord Jesus, who told Saul, "It is hard for you to kick against the goads" (Acts 9:4, NLT). Jesus used this imagery to show that Saul was hurting himself by persecuting Christians in resistance to God's will, just like stubborn oxen injure themselves when they kick at the sharp goads used by the farmer trying to get them to change direction. Similarly, humankind is only hurting itself as it continues to "kick against the goads" due to its selfish, broken nature – too proud to acknowledge its evil tendencies or even going so far as to excuse itself of those tendencies.

Through our unending lust and greed, we never stop warring with each other, the strong continue to take advantage of the weak, and many work to get rich at the expense of the poor. Through selfish neglect, we've polluted the air,[17] the earth,[18] and water sources,[19] upset the balance of nature to the extent that even the weather has been impacted,[20] and are generally in the pursuit of every kind of evil. You only have to turn on the news at any time of the day to see what I'm talking about. As a result, things continue to worsen for us and for all of creation.[21]

Despite Saul's deep-rooted commitment to persecute Christians out of existence, as a result of his encounter with Jesus that day on the road, he stopped kicking against the goads and was miraculously transformed, going on to become the Apostle Paul, one of the most influential persons in Christian history. You, too, can be transformed and come to know your true purpose as God intended, if you are willing.

Regarding the second point, God does indeed exist, and the evidence is presented to us every day, from within us, and through that which is all around us. From within us because, as the professor noted, we are wired to know him … we are wired for love, and he IS love (1 Jn. 4:8). This can be discerned if we're willing to open our hearts to him. But to do so, we must set aside our skepticism, contrary worldviews, and biases.

This is not just a mental exercise, a time of reflection, but one that requires us to delve earnestly into the seat of our souls where our thoughts, emotions, desires, and will define our true character by our decisions and actions. In so doing, God will reveal Himself to us just as He promised in Prov. 8:17, "I love those who love me; And those who diligently seek me will find me (NASB)." And he keeps his promises because "God is not a man, that He would lie" (Num. 23:19).

Asking you to set aside things you've clung to and relied upon for as long as you can remember may be a tall order, but consider the possibilities of taking this *road of transformation* that Saul found himself on. A road that leads you to become a newly created being with God himself living inside you (2 Cor. 5:17), a road that offers HIS PEACE through the PRINCE OF PEACE (Jn. 14:27), and gives you the joy of knowing you have eternal life in Him who is the Way and the Truth and the Life (Jn. 14:6; Rom. 6:23; 1 Jn. 5:11-12).

The evidence of God's existence is also through that which surrounds us, including the cosmos, because as noted earlier, "The heavens proclaim the glory of God. The skies display his craftsmanship. Day after day they continue to speak; night after night they make him known. They speak without a sound or word; [there is no speech or language where their voice is not heard.] Yet their message has gone throughout the earth, and their words to all the world (Ps. 19:1-4, NLT). Benson's Commentary explains it this way, "Their magnificent appearance, their exquisite order, their regular course, and their significant actions and operations, by which they declare their Author [is] no less intelligible than men [making] known their minds by their words,"[22] and are made available, day and night, for all living on earth to see and understand.

Moreover, the arachnid's persistent arguments about God's existence and power also mimic that of all of creation's awareness, as referenced earlier in Romans 8. Lastly, the professor argues that science (the discipline, not the worldview) was never a contradiction to the idea of God's existence or his role in all things created; on the contrary, it was influential and complementary in informing knowledge of that role.

The evidence presented in the first point is to convince you that your self-made plans and strategies for survival, without God, have been of no effect and have even made things worse. The second point is to open your eyes to the existence of God and his desire to have a personal relationship with you.

However, to have that relationship, the next steps are yours to take. The first of which is so simple that it confirms God's passion for us to be his children, as it relies on the principle of our free will to simply make a decision based on what we believe, and then act on it. It is the same principle as that found in Ps. 116:10, which says, "I believed in you, so I said … " In other words, it is what we BELIEVE and SAY that establishes that relationship. And what is that?!

"If you openly declare that JESUS IS LORD and believe in your heart that God raised him from the dead, you will be saved. For it is by believing in your heart that you are made right with God, and it is by openly declaring your faith that you are saved (Rom. 10:9-10).

The Apostle applied that principle and was transformed. Over the centuries that followed, millions have applied that principle. I have applied it. The greatest and most definitive victory you can achieve in this life is *eternal life through faith in Jesus Christ*. Don't let another day go by in a struggle you cannot win without Him. Make this day the day you also apply that principle and allow yourself to be transformed into a new creature in Christ Jesus with the love, joy, and peace that God always intended for you.

10

NOTES

1. 1 John 4:16, NLT.
2. 1 Cor. 13:4-7.
3. Deut. 30:19-20.
4. https://www.azquotes.com/quote/371808 Max Planck.
5. Jer. 29:13, Acts 17:27.
6. Ps. 19:1-4, Rom. 1:19-20.
7. Rom. 1:18.
8. Rom. 1:25, NIV.
9. Wave-Particle Duality Explained!; https://www.azoquantum.com/Article.aspx?ArticleID=614; https://www.rroij.com/open-access/waveparticle-duality-the-dual-nature-of-quantum-objects.pdf.
10. Superposition Position Explained (Schrodinger's Cat); Superposition and Wave-Particle Duality Explained!; Quantum Physics, Bill Carson, 2023.
11. Eph. 6:18.
12. Caroline M. Leaf. *Switch on your brain: the key to peak happiness, thinking, and health.* Paperback edition. Baker

Books. 2015, p. 121.
13. Prov. 23:7, NLV.
14. Eze. 28:17, NLT.
15. Matt. 28:18.
16. "These Spiders Build Decoy Dummies of Themselves" (Youtube)
17. Tiny and toxic: Researchers track smaller air pollution particles across US skies (2025, June 12) retrieved 14 June 2025 from https://phys.org/news/2025-06-tiny-toxic-track-smallerair.html; Air Pollution Charts & Graphs.
18. Chen H,Gao Band Li Y (2025) Soil Pollution and Remediation: emerging challenges and innovations. 13:1606054. Front. Environ. Sci. doi: 10.3389/fenvs.2025.1606054 2025 Chen, Gao and Li; https://www.explainthatstuff.co

19. https://www.usgs.gov/news/national-news-release/millions-us-may-rely-groundwater-contaminated-pfas-drinking-water; https://earthjustice.org/feature/map-coal-plants-failing-monitor-contaminated-water
20. https://www.msn.com/en-us/weather/other/ancient-carbon-emissions-from-rivers-may-accelerate-climate-change-study/ar-AA1GHDdR; https://wmo.int/publication-series/wmo-global-annual-decadal-climate-update-2025-2029.
21. Cvetković, V. M., Renner, R., Aleksova, B., & Lukić, T. (2024). Geospatial and Temporal Patterns of Natural and Man-Made (Technological) Disasters (1900–2024): Insights from Different Socio-Economic and Demographic Perspectives. *Applied Sciences*, *14*(18), 8129. https://doi.org/10.3390/app14188129; Man-Made Disaster Trends; Natural Disaster Trends.

22. https://biblehub.com/commentaries/benson/psalms/19.htm, refer to note for Psalm 19:4.

www.ingramcontent.com/pod-product-compliance
Lightning Source LLC
La Vergne TN
LVHW050610100826
845148LV00015B/3207